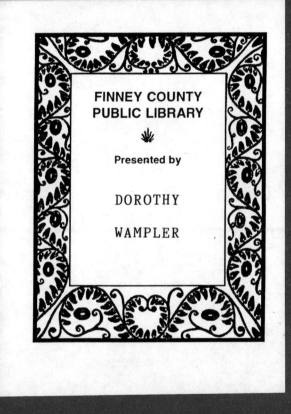

Young Mozart

BY Rachel Isadora

VIKING

VIKING
Published by the Penguin Group
Penguin Books USA Inc., 375 Hudson Street, New York, New York 10014, U.S.A.
Penguin Books Ltd, 27 Wrights Lane, London W8 5TZ, England
Penguin Books Australia Ltd, Ringwood, Victoria, Australia
Penguin Books Canada Ltd, 10 Alcorn Avenue, Toronto, Ontario, Canada M4V 3B2
Penguin Books (N.Z.) Ltd, 182–190 Wairau Road, Auckland 10, New Zealand

Penguin Books Ltd, Registered Offices: Harmondsworth, Middlesex, England

First published in 1997 by Viking, a division of Penguin Books USA Inc.

1   3   5   7   9   10   8   6   4   2

LIBRARY OF CONGRESS CATALOGING-IN-PUBLICATION DATA
Isadora, Rachel.
Young Mozart / by Rachel Isadora.
p.   cm.
Summary: A biography of the famous Austrian composer.
ISBN 0-670-87120-6 (hardcover)
1. Mozart, Wolfgang Amadeus, 1756–1791—Childhood and youth—Juvenile
literature. 2. Composers—Austria—Biography—Juvenile literature. [1. Mozart,
Wolfgang Amadeus, 1756–1791. 2. Composers.] I. Title.
ML3930.M9I83 1997 780′.92—dc20 [B] 96-5948 CIP AC MN

Manufactured in China
Set in Garamond No.3

For my mother and father

Wolfgang climbed up onto the chair in front of the clavier. He was too small to reach the keys, so he had to kneel. Nannerl, Wolfgang's older sister, listened as little three-year-old Wolfgang tried to play the piece she had just finished. When a note sounded right, Wolfgang laughed. But when a note sounded wrong, he burst out crying.

A year later, Papa Leopold, a musician himself, decided it was time to give four-year-old Wolfgang music lessons. In no time, Wolfgang had composed his first clavier concerto. The sheets of music were a mess of inkblots and smudges, but Papa Leopold could see that it was a very advanced piece. "It is so difficult no one could play it," he said. Wolfgang was writing music before he could write words.

At night, before falling asleep, Wolfgang played a bedtime game with Papa Leopold. He sang little tunes that he had thought up during the day. Papa Leopold listened carefully and made up a harmony to sing along. They sounded like two musical instruments. Wolfgang's tunes became more and more complicated, and soon Papa Leopold had to work to keep up. Wolfgang was learning very quickly.

One day Papa Leopold's fellow court musicians came to practice a piece he had composed for harpsichord and two violins. Wolfgang walked into the room holding a half-size violin. He too wanted to play. Papa Leopold told him that when he had taken violin lessons and learned to play, he could join them. Wolfgang began to cry. Johann Schachtner, feeling sorry for the little boy, invited Wolfgang to play along with him. The musicians began. Herr Schachtner played for a while, then stopped. Wolfgang played on. Everyone was amazed. Wolfgang had taught himself to play the violin! He played perfectly, and with great beauty. Papa Leopold listened with tears in his eyes.

Papa Leopold knew it was time to show the world his talented children. Wolfgang was five years old and Nannerl eleven when they left by coach for the city of Munich. There they performed for noblemen. The concert was a great success. Nannerl sang very well, but it was little Wolfgang who was the great sensation. The audience did not want him to stop playing. They called him a "wonderchild."

Wolfgang and Nannerl were invited to play for royalty in many cities of Europe. Everyone wanted to see them. Sometimes they were given money, sometimes gifts. After a concert before Empress Maria Theresa of Austria, Wolfgang tripped and fell. Little Princess Marie Antoinette, her daughter, rushed over to help him. When Wolfgang asked her to marry him, everyone burst into laughter. Wolfgang had no idea that this little girl was the future queen of France. Empress Maria Theresa was so delighted with Wolfgang and Nannerl that she presented each of them with a magnificent set of court clothes.

By the time Wolfgang was seven years old, he could compose music while he played it, without having to write it down first. "At present, four sonatas of M. Wolfgang Mozart are being engraved," wrote a very proud Papa. "Imagine the stir they will make when people find out they have been composed by a seven year old! God performs new miracles every day through this child." Wolfgang was happy. He was composing wonderful music and traveling with Nannerl, Mama, and Papa.

Wolfgang often became ill while on tour. His papa and mama thought Wolfgang was overworked and all he needed was a few months' rest. It is believed that Wolfgang suffered from a serious kidney disease. That explained why he was so small for his age. As soon as Wolfgang was well, travel to the great cities of Europe would begin again. He gave concerts in the afternoon and early evening and composed music in the morning and at night, sometimes working until dawn. By the time he reached the age of twenty-one, he had completed almost three hundred works!

In Vienna, Wolfgang fell in love with a girl named Constanze Weber. She was a lovely singer and fond of music. They were married and had six children; only two lived more than a year. Karl Thomas and Franz Xaver Wolfgang learned to play the clavier and loved to sing with their father, as Wolfgang had done with his own father years before. Sometimes their pet starling would join in.

Wolfgang earned a great deal of money, but he spent it quickly. He bought fine clothes for his family, gave big parties, and owned his own coach (which was a very extravagant thing to do). When Wolfgang was in great debt, he would teach, give concerts, and furiously compose one piece of music after another.

One day, Franz Joseph Haydn came to visit. He was considered the greatest composer of his day. He listened to Wolfgang. "Your son is the greatest composer I know," he told Papa Leopold. Though Haydn was twenty-four years older than Wolfgang, they became close friends.

By the time Wolfgang was twenty-nine years old, he had already composed several operas. But then he had an idea for a great opera that would be both funny and beautiful—*The Marriage of Figaro*. It was a success when first performed in Vienna, but in the city of Prague it was even more beloved. Everywhere Wolfgang and Constanze went, people were singing and dancing to tunes from *Figaro*. In gratitude, Wolfgang wrote the Prague Symphony. But most important, he was asked to write a new opera. He composed *Don Giovanni*.

One day a man named Emanuel Schikaneder came to Wolfgang with an idea for another opera. He would write the words and Wolfgang would write the music. *The Magic Flute* was a magic opera, and audiences loved it.

Wolfgang was composing great music, and Wolfgang and Constanze were happy. Then in July 1791 a stranger asked Wolfgang to write a requiem, a funeral mass. While composing the requiem, Wolfgang became very ill. Sometimes he thought he was writing the requiem for his own funeral.

On December 4, 1791, he asked friends to sing different parts of it with him at his bedside. On December 5, 1791, Wolfgang died, with the requiem unfinished. He was thirty-five years old.

1756-1791

Joannes Chrysostomus Wolfgangus Amadeus Mozart composed over six hundred pieces of music which are still treasured two centuries later by musicians and music lovers all over the world.

Mozart did not choose to become a musician; music was born in him.

Wolfgang Amadeus Mozart
learned to write music before he could
write words. By the age of five, he
had taught himself to play the violin,
and soon he was playing before the
crowned heads of Europe. By the time
Wolfgang was seven, he could compose music while he played it, and by
the age of twenty-one, after touring for
many years through Europe, he had
completed almost three hundred
works. He was the greatest composer
of his time, and many believe the
greatest who ever lived.

The story of Mozart's life, from his
childhood as an engaging prodigy
through the composing of his major
works and his early death, is recounted
by Caldecott Honor–winning artist
Rachel Isadora. Her brief, anecdotal
text combined with rich, detailed
watercolors bring Mozart's world to
vivid life in this infectious introduc-
tion to an extraordinary artist.